The Monkey King

The Monkey King

Inspired by Nazli Gellek

Adapted by Grania Davis

Illustrated by Sheila Johnson

DHARMA 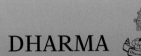 PUBLISHING

Color design by Dharma Publishing staff
Endpapers in casebound edition by Margie Horton

Library of Congress Cataloging-in-Publication Data
will be found at the end of this book.

Printed in the USA by Dharma Press, 2910 San Pablo Avenue,
Berkeley, California 94702

Dedicated to

children everywhere

The Jataka Tales

The Jataka Tales celebrate the power of action motivated by compassion, love, wisdom, and kindness. They teach that all we think and do profoundly affects the quality of our lives. Selfish words and deeds bring suffering to us and to those around us, while selfless action gives rise to goodness of such power that it spreads in ever-widening circles, uplifting all forms of life.

The Jataka Tales, first related by the Buddha over two thousand years ago, bring to light his many lifetimes of positive action practiced for the sake of the world. As an embodiment of great compassion, the Awakened One reappears in many forms, in many times and places, to ease the suffering of living beings. Thus these stories are filled with heroes of all kinds, each demonstrating the power of compassion and wisdom to transform any situation.

While based on traditional accounts, the stories in the Jataka Tales Series have been adapted for the children of today. May these tales inspire the positive action that will sustain the heart of goodness and the light of wisdom for the future of the world.

Tarthang Tulku   Founder, Dharma Publishing

Once upon a time in the Himalaya Mountains there lived a Great Being in the form of a monkey king. He was tall and strong and was always kind to his eighty thousand monkey subjects.

Nearby, on the bank of the Ganges River, there was a mango tree that gave such deep shade and had such thick leaves that it looked like a mountain top. Its fruit was wonderfully large and sweet and delicious. When it was ripe, some of the fruit fell on the ground, and some fell in the river.

One day the Monkey King was eating the fruit with the other monkeys. He looked out over the plains at the palace of Benares in the distance and thought, "Some day it will be dangerous for us when the mangoes fall in the water."

So he told his followers to pick all the fruit and flowers on the tree that grew over the river. But one mango was hidden by a bird's nest, and not one of the eighty thousand monkeys noticed it. There it stayed, growing large and ripe.

One day soon after, the Prince of Benares came to swim in the river with his retinue of wives, ministers, and servants. As he swam under the tree, the ripe mango fell down, right on top of his head!

"What is this fruit?" the prince cried in surprise.

"We don't know," said his wives, ministers, and servants.

"Then call the woodsman. He can tell us!"

The woodsman told the prince it was a mango. Sitting down under the tree, the prince cut up the beautiful yellow fruit and gave pieces first to the woodsman, then to his servants, his ministers, and his wives. Finally, when he was sure it was safe, he ate the rest himself. The flavor was so delicious that the prince was filled with desire for more of the wonderful fruit. Therefore, he stayed, eating ripe, juicy mangoes until he was full.

Then the servants built a fire, a guard was posted, and the prince lay down to sleep at the foot of the great tree.

At midnight, the Monkey King and his eighty thousand followers came to jump from branch to branch and eat the delicious fruit. Awakened by the chatter, the prince saw the monkeys and called his archers.

"Surround those monkeys," he said, "and don't let them escape. Tomorrow we will eat mangoes with roasted monkey meat!"

"Very well," said the archers, and they surrounded the tree.

The monkeys saw
that they could not
escape, and they were
frightened. They came
to the Monkey King,
shivering, and said,
"The tree is
surrounded by men
with huge bows and
sharp arrows! What
shall we do?"

"Don't be afraid," said their king, "I will save you."

So he stretched his own body as far as possible and made a bridge from the mango tree to a bamboo grove nearby. "Cross over my back quickly, and with good luck," he told the eighty thousand monkeys.

And so the monkeys escaped.

But the last monkey to cross over to safety was Devadatta, who was an enemy of the king. As he crossed, he jumped with all his might on the king's back. The Monkey King's heart broke, and he felt great pain. Devadatta left, and the king was all alone.

The prince watched all that happened. He thought, "This animal gave his own life to save his herd. It isn't right to kill this king of the monkeys. I will gently bring him down and take care of him."

So he had the Monkey King lowered on a smooth platform, and washed him in Ganges water. He rubbed the king with the finest oil, and gave him sweet drinks, and made a soft, fur bed for him.

Then the prince asked, "Why did you make a bridge for the other monkeys?"

And the Monkey King replied, "Because I am their king, and a good king must love his subjects." And so, throughout the rest of the night, the king taught the prince how to be a just ruler.

As the sun rose, the
Monkey King died of
his broken heart.
    The Prince of
Benares gave him a
wonderful funeral, with
flower garlands and
torches and incense
and golden offerings.
Then the prince went
home to Benares with
his wives, ministers,
and servants.

When he became king, he remembered the Monkey King's teachings and ruled kindly and wisely for the rest of his life.

My page

Colored by _____

Library of Congress Cataloging-in-Publication Data

Davis, Grania.
[King and the mangoes]
The monkey king / inspired by Nazli Gellek : adapted by Grania
Davis : illustrated by Sheila Johnson.
 p.   cm. -- (Jataka tales series)
Originally published under title: The king and the mangoes, c1975.

Summary: The Prince of Benares learns a valuable lesson from
the monkey king who gives his life to save his herd.

ISBN 0–89800–293–1. -- ISBN 0–89800–292–3 (pbk.)

1. Jataka stories, English.   [1. Jataka stories.]   I. Gellek,
Nazli.   II. Johnson, Sheila, ill.   III. Title.   IV. Series.
BQ1462.E5D386   1998
294.3'823--DC21
                                    98-2676   CIP   AC

The Jataka Tales Series

Golden Foot

Heart of Gold

A Precious Life

The Spade Sage

Three Wise Birds

The Monkey King

The Best of Friends

Courageous Captain

The King and the Goat

The Hunter and the Quail

The Proud Peacock and the Mallard

Great Gift and the Wish-Fulfilling Gem

A King, a Hunter, and a Golden Goose

The Rabbit Who Overcame Fear

The Value of Friends

The Magic of Patience

The Rabbit in the Moon

The Power of a Promise

The Parrot and the Fig Tree

The Fish King's Power of Truth